AF400816

Imperfect Solidarities

Aruna D'Souza

Imperfect Solidarities is the seventh installment of the Critic's Essay Series published by Floating Opera Press. Comprising long-form essays, the series gives voice to critics who offer thought-provoking ways in which to subvert or replace normative modes of discussing culture and the world beyond.

Other essays in the series:
Queer Formalism: The Return, by William J. Simmons
Remember the Details, by Skye Arundhati Thomas
After Institutions, by Karen Archey
Notes on Evil, by Steven Warwick
Perpetual Slavery, by Ciarán Finlayson
A Queer Theory of the State, by Samuel Clowes Huneke

To Priya, who keeps me honest

Contents

Grief, Fear, and Palestine, or Why Now?
9

I
Mistranslation and Revolution
27

II
Empathy and the Problem of Whiteness
39

III
Connecting through Opacity
52

IV
Leaving Difference Intact
68

Coda
Care before Love
81

Grief, Fear, and Palestine, or Why Now?

There are moments when different threads of your thinking, developed slowly over years, parallel and overlapping, eventually tie themselves into a knot. In my case, more than a decade of writing about empathy, translation, and mistranslation, the sovereign subject's right to opacity—and the question of how to forge solidarities while attending to these phenomena—suddenly became entangled, in my mind at least, with the horrors of genocide being played out in real time in Gaza.

On October 7, 2023, Hamas attacked villages and a music festival in southern Israel. Around 1,200 people—both Israeli and foreign civilians and Israeli security forces—were killed on that day, and 240 people were taken hostage. At the time of writing, in the first few months of 2024, more than 34,000 Palestinians have been killed, almost half of them children, and the vast majority of Gaza's infrastructure, including hospitals, schools, universities, and housing, has been destroyed.[1] The 1.3 million people who are sheltering in Rafah, in the south—initially designated a safe zone by Israel—are also now being massacred by the Israel Defense Forces (IDF), as Benjamin Netanyahu, the Israeli prime minister, presses forward with his military campaign there. Almost all aid into Gaza has been cut off, and Palestinians are starving. For anyone living in the United States, as I am, the siege is a decidedly domestic concern: the United States is Israel's strongest ally—financially and politically supporting the country in the form of military aid worth billions of dollars, consistently vetoing or watering down the United Nations Security Council's calls for a ceasefire—and is home to the largest Jewish population outside of Israel.[2]

The majority of Americans oppose Israel's actions in Gaza; that opposition has grown over the past six months,[3] and after seven foreign volunteers with World Central Kitchen, an NGO founded by the chef José Andrés, were killed on April 1, 2024, while delivering aid to Rafah, it has grown louder. Despite this, President Joe Biden has insisted that there is no red line that will lead to the United States cutting off military aid. But Biden's political brand—one that played a decisive role in beating Donald Trump in the 2020 presidential

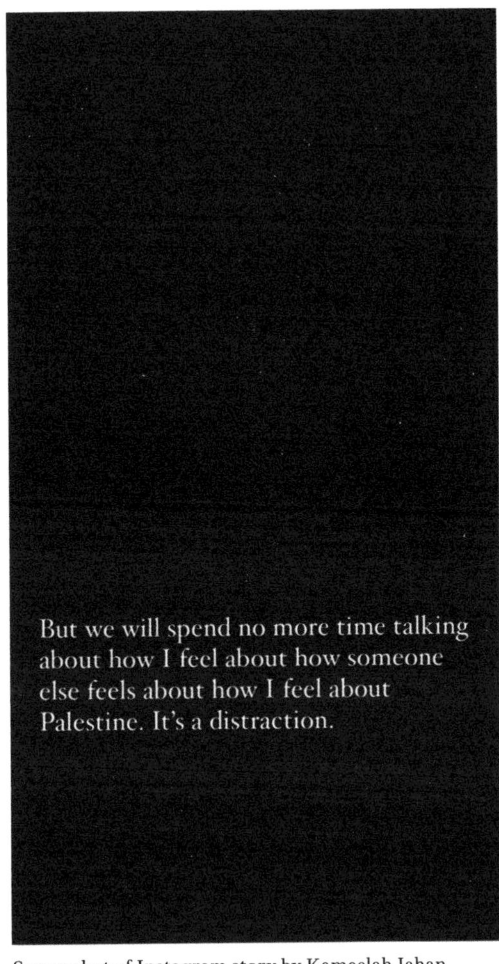

Screenshot of Instagram story by Kameelah Jahan
Rasheed, February 2024

election—is that he is an empathetic man. That selling point, on which he hopes to rely again in the upcoming election in November 2024, is on shaky ground, precisely because his empathy seems so selectively doled out. In his most directly critical admonishment of Israel to date, made on the occasion of the murder of these foreign aid workers, President Biden expressed dismay that "Israel has not done enough to protect civilians"[4]—as if the killing of 30,000 Palestinian civilians is just a matter of negligence, rather than a calculated strategy. He builds a pier to deliver aid to Rafah by sea at the same time as his administration increases the delivery of weapons to the country that is creating such a desperate need for aid in the first place. Yousef Munayyer, the head of the Palestinian-Israeli program at the Arab Center in Washington, DC, put the matter succinctly: "He has presented himself as this empath-in-chief; that is his great quality. And yet when it comes to Palestinian life, he just seems incapable of showing empathy to Palestinians."[5]

I watch this with horror; as a US taxpayer, I am funding the atrocities happening in Gaza every day. But my horror gives way to analysis, not only of the geopolitical situation itself, but of the way ordinary people are responding to what is unfolding. I am a social-media observer: I am deeply attuned to the ways in which language and interpretation appear and are reproduced around certain issues and events, ultimately framing the way that we all—individuals, policymakers, media, politicians, organizations—understand history in the making. Such language is at once a reflection of individual and collective sentiment and a driver of it, and, given how prevalent social media is in our informational landscape, it is also an algorithmic production. Our beliefs are shaped by what we see served up on our social-media feeds, by our favorite newspaper websites that put popular stories in easier-to-find places on their pages, by the memes that are shared in our WhatsApp and Signal groups.

But so are our emotional responses to the world. Anyone who's been on those apps in the past decade or so may recognize this to be true: while all of us have been focused recently on the capacity for these platforms to spread mis- or even disinformation, to misshape people's understanding of what is fact and what is fiction, it seems to me that the equally horrifying peril posed by social media is its capacity to (quite literally) create emotional responses in us. We've known this since at least 2014, when it was revealed that two years before, working with scientists who specialized in online behavior, Facebook manipulated the feeds of almost 700,000 users to create a phenomenon called "emotional contagion"—literally causing them to "catch feelings" from the posts they were seeing.[6] The subjects of the study did not give specific consent—their consent was contained within the soup-to-nuts user agreement they agreed to when they signed up for the service; and while the researchers' participation was limited to a week, it's clear that Facebook and other platforms continue to tweak their algorithms to encourage such responses.

Gaza is arguably the first genocide taking place on social media—we are seeing this happen in real time thanks to the many Palestinian journalists and civilians who have been documenting the violent onslaught as it has unfolded, and to the Israel Defense Forces (IDF) soldiers who have bizarrely, gleefully, and proudly posted their own transgressions on Instagram, TikTok, X (née Twitter), and Facebook. A number of those Palestinian journalists have become household names among young allies in the United States—Motaz Azaiza, Bisan Owda, Plestia Alaqad, and Wael al-Dahdouh, among others—and their reports are reposted by millions. In the face of a long, global history of the dehumanization of Arabs, of Muslims, of Palestinians—part and parcel of European colonialist enterprises, the United States' war on terror, and Israel's policies and actions—people circulate these images and reports of violence and cruelty in an attempt to encourage empathy with the victims of Israel's onslaught. They communicate their shock, their tears, their sense of grief, and encourage us to feel the same way in order to spur us to action. (Many others have done the same in response to the deaths of Israelis on October 7, and largely for the same reasons.)

This is, of course, a very understandable response to seeing human destruction on the scale that we're now witnessing. But the appeal to empathy (and its frequent correlate, outrage) is dangerous for a number of reasons. I want to telegraph those reasons in relation to the current conflagration in Gaza. They will also be explored in further depth, and in relation to artworks and literature as much as to geopolitics, in the subsequent chapters. When I speak of empathy, I'm talking about the capacity we possess—or believe ourselves to possess—of understanding and identifying what another person is going through.

So what could possibly be the problem with relying on such an essential human capacity to relate to the pain of others to inspire political change? First, it puts the burden on those being victimized to narrate their conditions in order to "change hearts and minds"—a horrible burden, especially for those who are reporting the violence while experiencing it in the most heinous ways. (Al-Dahdouh was broadcasting live on the ground in Gaza for Al Jazeera when he learned that his wife, seven-year-old daughter, fifteen-year-old son, and grandson had been killed in an Israeli airstrike; photos of him cradling the bodies of his family members circulated around the world.) Azaiza, who has been widely celebrated for his role in photographing the unfolding events in Gaza, having even been featured as 2023's Man of the Year by the Middle East edition of *GQ* magazine, has been clear about the effects of what he understands as his responsibility to bear witness—as well as about the ways he recognizes both the futility of enacting change even among those who seem to support his cause, and the extent to which he has fed the social-media monster. On February 28, 2024, he posted clips from an interview with the Turkish, English-language public broadcaster TRT World: "I'm not the content. What is happening in Gaza is not content for you. We are not telling you what is happening waiting for your likes, or views, or shares. No, we need you to act.…Like, people asking me 'What should we do?' Why are you asking me to tell you what to do? I'm the one who's dying there. You should know better."[7] On April 2, 2024: "I can't lose anyone anymore. I can't continue doing what I'm doing. Traveling from a place to another to raise more awareness while every moment my heart goes down when I see a picture for a friend of mine injured or dead. I am dead from inside and will not be able to continue."[8] Azaiza was only twenty-four years old when he was documenting the atrocities; we all have watched and shared videos from Palestinians even younger than him, mere children, begging the outside world to care for them. The fact is, we have constructed not only a social-media landscape but a political landscape in which we not only accept but demand such traumatic labor from those experiencing injustice so that we might dole out our attention.[9]

Second, the language of empathy is easily twisted, especially in a social-media context that encourages the spectacle of feelings above all else. The tearful confessional is a staple of TikTok and Instagram, and the language of empathy and care can be perverted in every direction. Two examples will suffice—but if you are active on social media, you will have seen hundreds or thousands more that follow suit. One is a post by actress Mayim Bialik on X, made on October 18, 2023, which adopted the language of open-hearted empathy to express sentiments that left almost no space to acknowledge the violence being visited on Palestinians:

> My heart is big. My heart can hold love for Israel, the homeland of the Jewish people. My heart feels the immense pain and horror the Israeli people are experiencing and I share that pain. My heart feels fear because of the anti-Semitism moving through this world with no end in sight. My heart feels rage for the lack of unanimous global support for a swift return of the hostages taken by Hamas, the terrorist organization terrorizing Israelis and Palestinians alike. My heart can hold all of this. Can yours?[10]

Another is Brett McGurk, coordinator for the Middle East and North Africa for the US National Security Council, who in mid-November 2023 gave a speech in which he

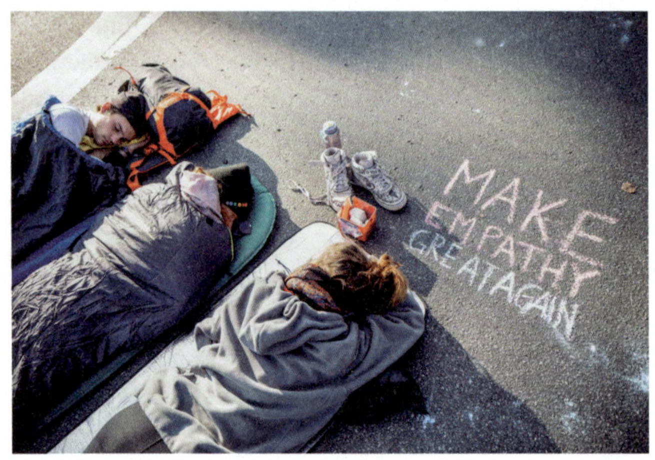

Participants in a blockade by the Extinction Rebellion climate movement at the start of the Block Berlin action week, with "Make empathy great again" written on the ground, October 7, 2019

justified the United States' failure to pressure Israel to rein in its indiscriminate bombing by saying, "We will not tell another country how to grieve."[11] It is breathtaking to consider the easy collapse of emotion (grief) and genocidal violence, an assertion that bombing is a form of grieving, and that Israeli grief must at all points be honored and centered even at the expense of Palestinian lives.

Third, it often privileges the emotional response of those doing the witnessing, instead of the real conditions being experienced by people on the ground. The artist Kameelah Jahan Rasheed pithily described the inanity of this phenomenon when she posted on Instagram on February 10, 2024, about a stranger who messaged her to talk her out of her position on Gaza: "But we will spend no more time talking about how I feel about how someone else feels about how I feel about Palestine." Again, this is tied up with the fact that in our age of political atomization—the increasing difficulty, in the wake of neoliberalism, to see ourselves as part of the multitude—we have been trained to focus on the self, on our individuality, identity, and brand, above all else. Empathy becomes the perfect tool for political expression in such a landscape because it is predicated on individual transformation rather than collective action.

There are other dangers, too, with posing empathy as a prerequisite to political solidarity. Those revolve around questions of who is worthy of such feeling. Attempts to "humanize" the victims of Israel's violence is predicated on the idea that their humanity is not a given but has to be argued for. But why should any of us—Palestinians least of all—be asked to prove a self-evident truth, especially when the decades-long dehumanization of Palestinians derives not from proof but instead from an ideological onslaught by Israel and its allies around the world. The attempts by peoples and governments to *dehumanize* should be treated as the problem requiring repair; instead, we put the burden on those who are being dehumanized to argue for their worthiness of empathy. (Let's also acknowledge here that the question of "humanity" as a precondition for care is already deeply suspect, especially in a world in which humans have wreaked havoc for millennia. Being human is no great shakes.)

In the face of an increased international opposition to Israel's actions, supporters of the two-state solution in the region—people who believe that Israel must continue to exist as a nation-state alongside an independent State of Palestine—have had to scramble: no longer can they rely on a majority in the United States or other Western countries to support unfettered military and financial aid. Thus, they have shifted the grounds of debate, portraying what's happening in Gaza as, essentially, a conflict between Benjamin Netanyahu and his Likud government on the one hand, and Hamas on the other, with Israeli and Palestinian civilians caught in the crossfire. Such a narrative allows us to pin the evil that has happened on two discrete entities, and—no matter what our assessment of the conflagration—empathize with, mourn, and celebrate the bravery and resilience of the innocents. (Senator Chuck Schumer's speech to the United States Congress on March 14, 2024—in which he called for elections in Israel in hopes that Netanyahu might be removed from power—took this tack precisely to bolster waning support for Israel—the need to stop the killing of Palestinians as a pure matter of human decency was a side issue at best.[12])

This process of constructing innocence is a way of avoiding harsh realities: that the situation of Palestinians was already untenable before Netanyahu rose to power and is a function of occupation itself, and that groups like Hamas, though not universally embraced by Palestinians by any means, did not emerge in a vacuum but rather are a consequence of seventy-five years of history in the region. The liberal mindset is not that different than the conservative one in that it needs to see conflict as a moral battle between good versus evil, or between perpetrators of violence versus victims of violence (each of these seen as fixed and immutable rather than contingent), and thus can only find empathy in the identification of and with pure innocence. Liberalism cannot abide the idea that liberation struggles are often bloody and messy, hence the seemingly constant demands in the early months of the conflagration that any criticism of Israel begin with a denouncement of Hamas violence. (It can, and does, fully accommodate the idea that collateral damage is to be entirely expected when in service of maintaining the power of the state, especially when that state is acting as an occupying or colonial force. The 30,000 Palestinians killed by Israel, maybe a few thousand of whom are in some way associated with Hamas, are described as unintended "civilian casualties." By contrast, every one of the Israelis murdered by Hamas on October 7 is understood to be the intended target of terrorism, even those who were killed by IDF bullets in the day's confusion.) We need, in turn, models of political action and accompanying discourse that allow us to acknowledge the discomforts on which solidarity must be based; the liberal desire to build bridges based on empathy are too shaky to withstand the complexities of our world.

And then there is the danger of getting into a rhetorical war predicated on whose tears are the biggest, most sincere, most deeply felt, most legitimate. Black women and other women of the global majority have long known the danger of "white lady tears"—the moment when a white woman cries, all rational discussion, and certainly any discussion of justice, goes out the window.[13] The feelings of the white individual are centered at the expense of the needs of the group. Likewise, now, tears that trace their legacy to the horrors of the Holocaust outweigh tears that trace theirs to the injustice of the first Nakba.

By asking that we consider forms of solidarity that exist beyond empathy, I am not saying that we should transform ourselves instead into perfectly rational, data-driven beings untouched by our emotions. I do not believe that such a being exists, nor do I think that living in an utterly rationalistic world would be any better than the one we live in now. Rather, I am asking that we consider how empathy functions not necessarily as a bridge-building tool in the creation of alliances, but rather allows us to *avoid* the hard work of facing our biggest problems, by having us turn inward, into the ego-driven space of emotion. Just as Sigmund Freud described the process of transference—the process wherein a patient projects deep, intense, and unconscious feelings, including those of "love," onto her analyst—as a form of avoidance, an excuse to evade the deep, soul-shattering realities of trauma, empathy allows us to distract ourselves from action, or at least defer it (sometimes endlessly) until our need to understand and relate to others' pain is satisfied.

To be clear: my observations in these and the following pages are not an argument that we shouldn't feel, deeply, the violence and injustice that we see in the world. We should. Rather, I ask that we question whether a politics based on an emotional identification with others—on empathy—will save us. Can empathy get us where we need to go? This book is a tentative gesture toward thinking beyond such forms of political connection, toward asking whether or not solidarity can coalesce before or beyond understanding each other. What results is a picture of what an *imperfect solidarity* might look like—one based on temporary, context-specific alliances, one that allows difference and even contradiction to remain intact, and that sees such contradiction as a strength, not a weakness. I dream of a world in which we act not from a love of our fellow humans (and, for that matter, nonhumans), but from something much more difficult: an obligation to care for each other whether or not we empathize with them.

My argument is, at best, glancing—coming at these questions from different, maybe even tangential, angles—and I don't offer a roadmap for what's next. This may be a failure of argumentation, but I prefer to see it as a demonstration of the kind of thinking for which I'm advocating—one in which the friction produced by multiplicity produces a spark, and that spark starts a fire. I explore what for me are interrelated concepts: empathy, of course, but also translation (of languages, of the self into the terms of the other); the relationship of empathy to power, and especially the power afforded by whiteness; the right of every sovereign subject to opacity (i.e., the right not to translate oneself into hegemonic terms). All of my thinking has developed from looking at art and literature—from Amitav Ghosh's novel *Sea of Poppies* to Felix Gonzalez-Torres, Stephanie Syjuco, and Candice Breitz, to an important exhibition curated by the artists Ana Mendieta, Zarina, and Kayuko Miyamoto. These examples, I hope, ground my thinking.

1   As of April 2024, the death count has remained at just upwards of 34,000, but that is more due to the fact that the Palestinian authorities have lost the capacity to count the dead, rather than a cessation of casualties.
2   Jonathan Masters and Will Merrow, "U.S. Aid to Israel in Four Charts," Council on Foreign Relations, January 23, 2024, https://www.cfr.org/article/us-aid-israel-four-charts (accessed March 9, 2024); Michelle Nichols, "US Blocks Ceasefire Call with Third UN Veto in Israel–Hamas War," Reuters, February 20, 2024, https://www.reuters.com/world/us-casts-third-veto-un-action-since-start-israel-hamas-war-2024-02-20/ (accessed March 9, 2024).
3   Jeffrey M. Jones, "Majority in U.S. Now Disapprove of Israeli Action in Gaza," GALLUP, March 27, 2024, https://news.gallup.com/poll/642695/majority-disapprove-israeli-action-gaza.aspx#:~:text=Approval%20has%20dropped%20from%2050%25%20to%2036%25%20since%20November&text=WASHINGTON%2C%20D.C.,actions%2C%20while%2036%25%20approve (accessed April 8, 2024).
4   "Statement from President Joe Biden on the Death of World Central Kitchen Workers in Gaza," The White House, April 2, 2024, https://www.whitehouse.gov/briefing-room/statements-releases/2024/04/02/statement-from-president-joe-biden-on-the-death-of-world-central-kitchen-workers-in-gaza/ (accessed April 11, 2024).
5   David E. Sanger and Peter Baker, "Biden Is 'Outraged.' But Is He Willing to Use America's Leverage with Israel?" *The New York Times*, April 3, 2024, https://www.nytimes.com/2024/04/03/us/politics/biden-israel-gaza.html (accessed April 11, 2024).
6   "Emotional Contagion," Wikipedia, last modified March 8, 2024, https://en.wikipedia.org/wiki/Emotional_contagion#:~:text=Emotional%20contagion%20is%20a%20form,ways%2C%20both%20%20implicitly%20or%20explicitly (accessed April 11, 2024).

7   TRT World (@trtworld) and Motaz Azaiza (@motaz_azaiza), Instagram, February 28, 2024, https://www.instagram.com/reel/C35cQK2oiuB/?igsh=MXM2ZXA4cXJ1NDFxaQ== (accessed April 11, 2024).

8   Motaz Azaiza (@motaz_azaiza), Instagram, April 2, 2024, https://www.instagram.com/p/C5RAHyvrD9f/?igsh=NHZmdWRvYWFkbHBv (accessed April 11, 2024).

9   One might note the responses to the social media–driven #MeToo movement, in which people were encouraged to share their traumatic experiences of sexual assault online in order to generate awareness and empathy, or the #BlackLivesMatter movement, which elicited a similar response from those who had experienced anti-Black racism. Both were predicated on the idea that people didn't truly realize the extent of the suffering caused by misogyny and anti-Blackness, but in both cases it was hard not to feel like we were exploiting the already exploited to demonstrate something we should all be aware of already.

10   Mayim Bialik (@mixxmayim), X, October 18, 2023, https://x.com/missmayim/status/1714706170693513609 (accessed April 8, 2024).

11   Brett McGurk, "Remarks at the IISS Manama Dialogue, First Plenary Session, Saturday 18 November 2023," https://www.iiss.org/globalassets/media-library---content--migration/files/manama-dialogue-delta/2023/final/p1/waleed-elkhereiji---deputy-minister-of-foreign-affairs-saudi-arabia_as-delivered.pdf (accessed April 8, 2024). Shortly after the Hamas attack, the writers Joshua Leifer and Gabriel Winant debated the way grief has long been instrumentalized by the Israeli state, and how such instrumentalization complicated the response to the deaths on October 7. See Joshua Leifer, "Toward a Humane Left," *Dissent*, October 12, 2023, https://www.dissentmagazine.org/online_articles/toward-a-humane-left/ (accessed April 9, 2024). Gabriel Winant, "On Mourning and Statehood: A Response to Joshua Leifer," *Dissent*, October 13, 2023, https://www.dissentmagazine.org/online_articles/a-response-to-joshua-leifer/ (accessed April 9, 2024).

12   The full text of Schumer's speech is available here: "Majority Leader Schumer Calls on Israeli Government to Hold Elections," Senate Democrats, March 14, 2024, https://www.democrats.senate.gov/news/press-releases/majority-leader-schumer-calls-on-israeli-government-to-hold-elections (accessed April 8, 2024).

13   Ruby Hamad, "How White Women Use Strategic Tears to Silence Women of Color," *The Guardian*, May 7, 2018, https://www.theguardian.com/commentisfree/2018/may/08/how-white-women-use-strategic-tears-to-avoid-accountability (accessed April 10, 2024).

I
Mistranslation and Revolution

Empathy is a concept based, at its heart, on understanding—it depends on the ability to translate the experience of another into one's own language. How often have we heard calls to put ourselves in someone else's shoes, in an effort to see something from another's perspective? In a moment when so many of us are hoping for a degree of revolution—some change, to whatever extent, in the increasingly impossible conditions of life on this planet—it feels like everyone, from politicians to educators to museum directors, have argued that increased empathy is a means to such an end.

In the United States, this has been especially true since the 2016 presidential election, when liberal pundits realized with horror how many people were willing to vote for an outspoken white supremacist, misogynistic, homophobic, transphobic, ableist, and otherwise hateful man, and doubled down on the idea that empathy was the key to a more progressive political arena. As it had been during Hillary Clinton's campaign, "love trumps hate" became the postelection rallying cry, a slogan that placed the personal obligation to understand each other at the heart of a politics of resistance.[1] It has continued to serve as a banner under which this so-called resistance organized in the wake of Donald Trump's inauguration and during his presidency. It was premised on the idea that a greater understanding of the experiences of marginalized people would lead the United States to a more perfect justice, more humane political leaders, fairer laws and less bias in punishment, fewer police shootings of Black and brown people, and less racism generally in our daily lives. As we face another election in which Trump is the Republican candidate against Joe Biden—a man supporting a genocide in Gaza by supplying seemingly unlimited money and weapons to Israel, while publicly expressing dismay at the loss of civilian life, painting himself as empathetic above all else and channeling sentiments of kindness and respect in his rhetoric—I expect that the value of empathy will once again be held up as a political asset.

Empathy is one of the things that makes us human and is a deeply important quality to cultivate. The problem with imagining it as a useful tool for political transformation, however, is twofold, as the example of anti-Black racism demonstrates. First because, as historians have shown, racism did not come before institutions—institutions created the need for racism. The racialization of Black Africans happened in order to justify slavery—white Europeans had to argue that dark-skinned Africans were something less than fully human in order to rationalize treating them as such. Slavery was not the product, but the origin, of racism. As institutions such as slavery continued to structurally place Black and darker-skinned people in a debased position, racism became naturalized, practically invisible. Now, hundreds of years into the project of white supremacy, we must not fall into the trap of imagining that changing attitudes—cultivating empathy for the oppressed—will undo structures. The structures need to be undone in order to clear the conceptual and imaginative space for empathy to flourish.

The second problem with considering empathy as a viable political tool is simply this: I don't want to wait for people to develop empathy for me until I am treated as a full human being. I don't want your life to depend on my capacity for understanding, either. Empathy is a personal transformation, not necessarily a collective act—it replaces political revolution with atomized notions of individuals doing right by others. And when it is the basis for collective action, it can do as much harm as good. After all, in an earlier moment of globalization, the colonizing projects of European empires and the Catholic Church were motivated, or at least justified, by empathy—by wanting to save people from their own darkness. A politics based on empathy imagines justice as something to be bestowed by newly enlightened individuals on other, lesser individuals and communities. If there is a politics in empathy, it is one that allows the person called on to be empathetic to remain in a position of supremacy, doling out justice as a matter of kindness—or, perhaps, pity.

The opposite of empathy, one of them at least, is a failure to comprehend the other. This sounds like a terrible thing, perhaps, but I want to think about the possibilities of a politics that can accommodate, even thrive on, incomprehensibility. In thinking through this problem, I turn to one of my favorite novels: Amitav Ghosh's *Sea of Poppies*, published in 2008. Is it possible, the author asks, to build an epic story around the very problem of linguistic and cultural opacity: Can we imagine a situation in which the Tower of Babel could be built, in which cooperation could occur even in the face of the cacophony of languages spoken by its builders? What, that is to say, are the narrative possibilities of mistranslation?[2] And, as a not-insignificant corollary, what are the revolutionary possibilities of mistranslation?

The reach of the novel—the first of a trilogy that includes *River of Smoke* (2011) and *Flood of Fire* (2012)—spans the early nineteenth-century globe, a period when the opium trade was fueling the British economy and mapping geopolitics. The story follows the *Ibis*, a ship that has made its way from the Americas, where it has picked up a free Black man passing for white along with goods produced by enslaved laborers on plantations, to England, where raw materials are dropped off and new merchandise laded, around the coast of Africa, across the Indian Ocean, and eventually to Calcutta. The opium being cultivated by sharecroppers in Bengal will, it is planned, eventually be dropped off in China, against the wishes of that country's leaders who rightly see it as a means by which their citizens are made docile and beholden to European colonialists. Along the way, the ship adds and sheds crew, who are known collectively as lascars (a word that implies something like "pirate")—a hodgepodge of Europeans, Africans, Chinese, South Asians, and Black people from North America and the Caribbean. Out of the many languages each speak, they forge a common(ish) parlance—lascari English, a pidgin dialect, full of loanwords and salty curses and the necessary lingo to keep the ship afloat. It is, the book's narrator tells us, "a motley tongue, spoken nowhere but on the water, whose words were as varied as the port's traffic, an anarchic medley of Portuguese calaluzes and Kerala

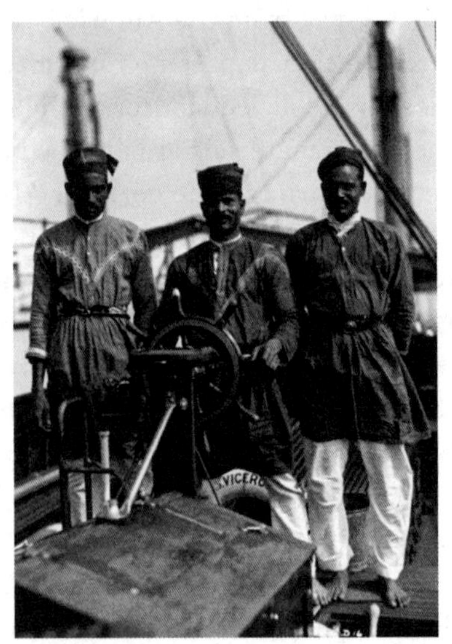

Three lascars on the RMS *Viceroy of India*,
1930–1939

pattimars, Arab booms and Bengal paunch-ways, Malay proas and Tamil catamarans, Hindusthani pulwars and English snows—yet beneath the surface of this farrago of sound, meaning flowed as freely as the currents beneath the crowded press of boats."[3] It is a language, in other words, tied not to land or country but to movement, migration, trade routes, and the space between.

When the ship arrives in Calcutta, the global port city does not disappoint, linguistically speaking: Ghosh introduces here Bengali peasants who are eking out an existence under the thumb of opium traders, a French botanist and his India-born daughter, who is more comfortable wearing saris and speaking the local dialects than wearing dresses and conversing in her mother tongue, muckety-mucks and functionaries in the British East India Company, and an elegant, well-educated maharajah. Each speaks, or fails to speak, any common dialect. Even the Englishmen—who claim to have a monopoly not just on opium but on civilization itself—use a form of English that has been so transformed (enriched? mangled?) by Britain's imperial adventures that it is barely recognizable to the reader. The maharajah employs language that perhaps sounds to readers' ears most like our own, but this ability to communicate with us does not grant him any special power, as he is consistently misunderstood by the English businessmen who have fixed the rules of the game and who hear only through the lens of their arrogance, greed, and self-interest. Language here lacks transparency and reveals itself as a maze or an obstacle course rather than a smooth pathway to human connection.

What makes this book illuminating, to my mind, is the author's refusal to translate—we are left to muddle our way through the dialogue in the same way as the characters, understanding wisps and threads without any feeling of fluency. The only way of comprehending what is happening is to abandon the frustration that might come from not being delivered a fictional world fully available to us and instead to float on the language the way a ship might float on the water.

Sitting with incomprehension is an uncomfortable act—for those of us whose mother tongue is English, it is also an unfamiliar one, given the way in which our preferred system of communication has been imposed on the world. But in *Sea of Poppies*, our discomfort isn't futile. Even if we don't understand everything, we end up understanding enough to follow, and ultimately enjoy, the story. Likewise, even when the sailors and rulers and colonials and peasants interpret based on an imperfect grasp of what others are saying—sometimes wildly misreading a speaker's intent—this creates no impediment to the narrative. The story goes on, ending with an event that will change all of their lives: the characters are forced, coerced, or gathered willingly on the *Ibis* for various purposes (to travel toward freedom or indentured labor, by turns), an uprising occurs in the face of injustice, and people escape in multiple directions. The endless misunderstandings contained in the saga create spaces where characters are able to insert their own desires and urgencies and move forward together, even if that movement is neither synchronized nor singular. Revolution is sketched here as a form of misprision.[4]

In a similar vein, the artist Kameelah Jahan Rasheed speaks of the "leaky sentence"—a form of communication in which meaning spills out, overflows, cannot be contained. If the sentence is a device that holds unruly words together, a leaky sentence maintains the unruliness. If the sentence is an atomized form of order, the leaky sentence represents disorder. If the mobility promised by global capitalism depends upon containerization—being able to carry things in an efficient, contained way—the leak is inefficiency, that which slows down and resists such a shuttling of people and their labor across the world.

The *Ibis* doesn't leak as such. A leaky boat is its own sort of problem. But it leaks in other ways: it sloughs people, depositing them around the world, sometimes against their best interests (as in the case of indentured laborers), at other times against the will of the shipowner (as in the case of stowaways, or of the lascars who regularly disappear once their pockets are lined with earnings). Ports are some of the leakiest geographic sites, places where borders become porous and often unpoliceable, no matter how much one tries to fortify them.

The Calcutta that Ghosh describes in *Sea of Poppies* is indeed a place of leakage. Here, languages slosh around, mix and dissolve, traded goods get filched, people appear and disappear. Time passes: history is made, unmade, re-made. The book asks us to imagine ourselves in a world with only the slightest wisp of a common language—an English that has been forced by its speakers in myriad directions and has been infiltrated by many other tongues, thanks to colonialism and trade. And yet, even in this chaos, solidarities emerge—momentary alliances based not on empathy but on imperfect understandings of others' motivations, desires, or values. This is especially apparent in relation to Zachary, the free Black man who allows himself to be taken for white. He is embraced both as an ally of the lascar seamen, who see his success as a subversion of the power of the white boat captain who is not privy to his true racial identity, as well as by the white characters in the book, who understand him to be an unusually effective mediator with recalcitrant characters of color. He, meanwhile, embraces both these roles and functions. Momentary alliances based on imperfect understandings: this seems to me the most important lesson of the book, given the times in which we live, in which we find living under the conditions of late capitalism and creeping fascism untenable. We have become so divided and atomized, so individualized by the logic of neoliberalism, that empathy has been made nearly impossible and its future attainment has become a deferral of revolution—change will come when we understand each other better—rather than a means transformation in the now.

To come back to the issue of language, it also hinges on an impossibility. Just as some part of meaning gets lost in translation, so do parts of ourselves as we are forced to translate our sense of being into another language or definition of personhood. This is the violence at the heart of becoming a psychological subject that Jacques Lacan elaborated three-quarters of a century ago—and it is a process that requires us to submit ourselves inevitably to the authority of a governing language (also known, in Lacanian terms, as the law). Empathy doesn't account for that which overflows the translation of the other into the terms of the self. It works to contain or, if containing fails, to reject that excess.

Communication through the thicket of mistranslation is an act of generosity. To be able to act together without full comprehension, to be able to float on the seas of change: What would a politics based on that capacity look like?

1   This discussion of empathy as a solution to racism is borrowed from
    my 2018 book *Whitewalling: Art, Race, and Protest in 3 Acts*, published
    by Badlands Unlimited.
2   Amitav Ghosh, *Sea of Poppies* (New York: Farrar, Straus, and Giroux,
    2009). For a fuller discussion of this novel, see my essay "Sea of
    Poppies and the Possibilities of Mistranslation," in *Traduttore,
    Traditore*, ed. Karen Greenwalt and Katja Rivera, exh. cat. Gallery
    400 (Chicago: University of Illinois Chicago, 2017).
3   Ghosh, *Sea of Poppies*, 108.
4   Harold Bloom, in his classic work of literary theory *The Anxiety of
    Influence* (1973), described the ways in which younger poets opened a
    creative space for themselves through a process of "misprision"—
    a willful misreading of the poetry of their elders. In a sense, Bloom
    was recognizing the way that mistranslation, misreading, and
    misunderstanding are not just failed attempts to translate, read, or
    understand, but, indeed, can be generative and creative acts—
    acts that make new forms of enunciation, new languages, possible.
    Harold Bloom, *The Anxiety of Influence: A Theory of Poetry*,
    2nd ed. (Oxford: Oxford University Press, 1997).

II
Empathy and the Problem of Whiteness

If empathy demands of those experiencing injustice that we narrate our trauma in the language of the majority, we need to attend to the ways in which that majority is often white, wealthy, and powerful. We must ask ourselves if cultivating empathy, or placing empathy at the center of our understanding of building solidarity, merely reifies the very inequalities we want to dismantle. This question lies at the heart of a project by Candice Breitz called *Love Story* (2016), in which she challenged audiences to question their own tendency to center whiteness (and, even more pointedly, white celebrity) when faced with the often-unimaginable horrors of forced migration.

On March 5, 2012, social media blew up in response to a short documentary about Joseph Kony, a Ugandan war criminal and the head of the Lord's Resistance Army, a militia group that conscripted children as soldiers. "Kony 2012" was the first video that could truly be described as viral (receiving upward of thirty million views per day when it initially released), and in short order a host of celebrities—including George Clooney, Angelina Jolie, Oprah Winfrey, Taylor Swift, Justin Bieber, and Kim Kardashian, among many others—signed on to the (white) filmmakers' campaign to track down the fugitive Kony and bring him to justice. Though it inspired a tidal wave of newborn "clicktivists"—online activists who were not involved in on-the-ground organizing or sustained engagement with the issue beyond their digital outrage—the video was criticized by a wide range of scholars and NGOs working on the African continent. According to these critics, "Kony 2012" was guilty of oversimplifying the hugely complex dynamics through which child soldiers are recruited and exploited, instead putting forward a series of digestible soundbites for easy consumption by Western viewers, most of whom were likely unable to identify Uganda on a map. The viral footage's stripped-down account portrayed Kony as the singular perpetrator of a range of violent human rights violations, without acknowledging the historical and structural conditions that formed the backdrop to these abuses, conditions that stemmed largely from the West's devastating colonial exploitation of the region. In focusing so much attention on a single evil African warlord, social-media commentators were conveniently choosing to forget the West's own crimes against humanity, instead doubling down on a racist narrative in which Africa was (yet again) framed as a dark continent that needed to be saved from itself.

It was in this context that the Nigerian American novelist Teju Cole sent out a series of tweets that, in the pithiest but most devastating terms, described a phenomenon he refers to as "the White-Savior Industrial Complex."[1] "The white savior supports brutal policies in the morning, founds charities in the afternoon, and receives rewards in the evening," read one. "The White Savior Industrial Complex is not about justice. It is about having a big emotional experience that validates privilege," read another.[2]

The brilliance of Cole's formulation was the collision of two seemingly unrelated terms. The first is a long-standing trope in Western thought, "the white savior complex"—known historically as "the white man's burden"—a belief that, since white people were more civilized, they had a moral obligation to serve humanity by rescuing darker-skinned people from their own ignorance and savagery. The second is the concept of the military-industrial complex. With this deft wordplay, Cole underlines the way in which a particular form of white supremacy continues to voraciously amass capital while satisfying the egocentric belief among even the most liberal-minded white people that they have the answers to the world's problems. If that capital took the form of captured land, people, and economic profit during the era of colonization and the slave trade, it has persisted in multiple ways since: as money, yes, but also as cultural capital—brutal policies in the morning, charities in the afternoon, rewards in the evening. Never has "wanting to make the world a better place" come under such well-earned scrutiny.

The question of empathy and its imbrication in white supremacy culture (which is to say, the culture in which most of us, whether in Europe or settler-colonial or post-colonial nations, live): this is what I want to explore. Breitz's *Love Story* (2016) delves into the same nexus of issues that Cole telegraphed in his tweetstorm. The work is designed to be installed in two rooms: a larger, darkened, cinematic space with a smaller chamber behind.[3] In the first space, one is confronted with a large-scale projection that alternates between appearances by Hollywood stars Julianne Moore and Alec Baldwin. Each is shown sitting in director's chairs against a green screen backdrop on a set that reveals the accoutrements of a film shoot—lights, reflectors, overhead mics. In successive cuts, they speak directly to the camera in a disarmingly intimate way. It is hard not to be starstruck, gazing at Moore's aging, unadorned, and undeniably beautiful face, or hearing Baldwin's rumbling baritone, but for all the

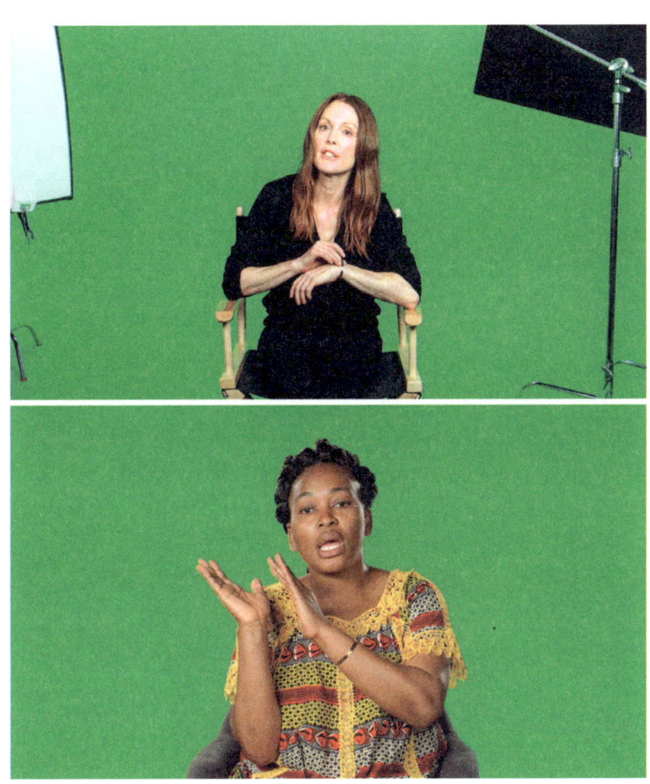

Candice Breitz, *Love Story* (2016), video still

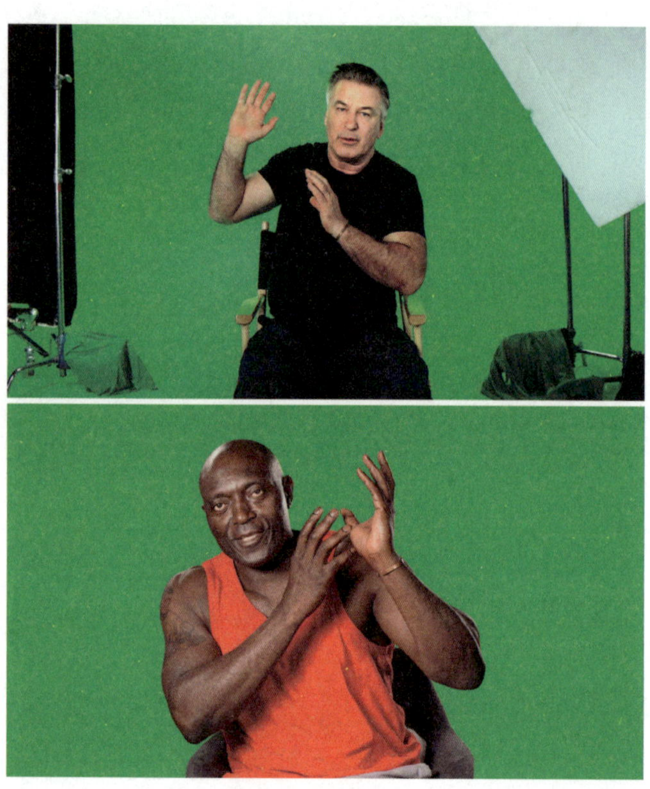

Candice Breitz, *Love Story* (2016), video still

glittering fantasy of their celebrity personae, the words coming out of their mouths point to terrible realities.

Despite the confessional demeanor of the actors and the intimate access suggested by the camera's framing, it becomes clear over the seventy-three-minute montage that the anecdotes related by the stars are not their own, or even that of singular characters. Rather, these personal narratives are borrowed from a range of displaced individuals, each recounting the abuses and sometimes outright horrors they have experienced in their countries of origin, events that prompted them to undertake perilous journeys across borders and into countries that too often received them with hostility. Baldwin and Moore, here voluntarily ceding Hollywood's tools-of-the-trade (costumes, makeup, assumed accents, props, and scenery) nonetheless manage to convey through an affective shorthand the distinguishing characteristics of each subject via gestures, posture, idiosyncratic movements, and vocal rhythms. Beyond these aspects of the actors' craft, it is only via the subtle use of personal accessories (a brooch, a bracelet, sunglasses, et cetera) that we can identify which refugee is speaking at any given moment in this tightly edited script.

In the second space, six flatscreen monitors offer access to the original interviews from which the fragments performed by Moore and Baldwin are drawn. Here is an opportunity, should one wish to take it, to hear firsthand from asylum seekers Shabeena Francis Saveri, a South Asian transgender woman; Luis Nava Molero, a Venezuelan dissident who refused to shy away from criticizing Hugo Chávez; Farah Abdi Mohamed, a Somali atheist; Mamy Maloba Langa, a Congolese woman who was the victim of unimaginable sexual violence as a consequence of her husband's changing political fortunes; José Maria João, an Angolan man who was exploited as a child soldier; and Sarah Ezzat Mardini, a competitive swimmer who made the perilous Mediterranean crossing by boat to escape Syria's civil war. The first-person interviews were conducted in Cape Town, Berlin, and New York, the cities in which the interviewees have sought refuge. Each interviewee sits against the same green screen backdrop that framed Moore and Baldwin.

When the actors appeared on a similarly pared-down set, it had the air of being "industry standard." But now, re-encountering it as a backdrop for interviews with people who have been violently displaced, it is hard not to think about the green screen as a provisional backdrop that allows the setting to be inserted after the fact. Here, green screen signifies "placelessness," a filmic limbo that operates as a metaphor for forced migration itself.[4] Each interview runs for three to four hours, making it impossible to experience this archive in its entirety, without returning to the museum over the course of multiple days.

Collectively, the interviews are infinitely more varied and nuanced than the readings offered by Moore and Baldwin, despite the actors' virtuoso channeling of their individual subjects. As we watch, a slow realization emerges: Hollywood can never fully capture the complexity of human experience. The interviewees' unpolished accounts are more interesting, particular, and textured than any fictional portrayal might convey—and, yet, these two actors have seduced us into thinking otherwise. It is a *Wizard of Oz* moment—we have seen the reality behind the curtain, and the spectacle is diminished.

On an immediate level, *Love Story* addresses one of the most urgent geopolitical crises of our times—the virtually unprecedented displacement of people under pressures of war, famine, economic privation, environmental disaster, political oppression, and other forms of violence (108.4 million as of 2022, according to the UN,[5] more than thirty-five million of whom are classified as refugees; that number is undoubtedly much higher now, given recent events in Gaza, Sudan, and the Democratic Republic of Congo). But the work is equally concerned with the mechanisms through which political consciousness around such issues is generated. While we may have been genuinely moved by Moore's and Baldwin's renditions of the lives of their subjects, when confronted with the full-length interviews in the second space of the installation, we begin to recognize

Love Story's conceit as one of whitewashing, an all-too-familiar strategy in the entertainment industry in which stories that properly belong to people of color are rendered "relatable"—worthy of our empathy and care, available for our psychic identifications—by casting white actors or centering white characters. The practice is most often justified as an attempt to garner "mainstream appeal"—in other words, the attention of white audiences who are presumed not to care about people who do not look like them. (Though examples abound, one stands out in its audacity and cynicism: in a recent interview, Gregory Allan Howard, screenwriter of the film *Harriet*, revealed that when he first started to shop around the idea for a movie about the Black antislavery activist in the early 1990s, a studio executive suggested casting Julia Roberts as Harriet Tubman.[6] Apocryphal, perhaps, but also telling.)

As we listen carefully to the excerpted interview fragments that the white actors ventriloquize, Breitz constantly draws our attention to the dubious operations of ginning up empathy by centering white subjectivity: as when Baldwin-as-José Maria João, the former child soldier from Angola, says that "[t]he media is only interested in famous people; I don't think all those nice people would come just to listen to my story"; or when Moore-as-Mamy Maloba Langa, the Congolese woman who fled sexual violence, remarks that "[p]eople don't even care about us, you know, they would never put us on a movie screen and talk about us." It is hilarious and poignant, heart-wrenching and cringe-inducing all at once to see the actors mouthing the migrants' admissions that they don't really know who the actors are, declaring their hope that the world will listen if famous people tell their stories, expressing their belief in the power of celebrity to advance political causes, revealing their starstruck-ness, or—in the case of the Venezuelan academic and political dissident Luis Ernesto Nava Molero—railing against the Hollywoodization of the public sphere and our mindless manipulation by movie stars.[7]

Breitz herself is realistic, in commenting on *Love Story*, about the tendency of privileged white audiences to respond more readily to stars who look (and sound) like them: "It's naïve and unproductive to assume that you can automatically get people to sit down and spend time ingesting and reflecting on complex stories that are completely removed from their experience. Especially in an attention economy in which we're increasingly so-cialized into a fast-forward relationship with endless streams of information."[8] This is not to say that she is sanguine about such internalized bias—or wants us to be. The structure of *Love Story* allows us to confront our own capacities (or lack thereof) for paying attention within an image economy that is constantly trying to solicit our gaze (hustling to "get our eyeballs").

What Breitz's work shows us is that it's often all too easy to empathize with someone due to the color of their skin or notoriety, or for any number of other reasons that seem pretty clearly at odds with the idea of universal justice. It's discomfiting to think that something that we understand to be an essential human quality like empathy could be so imbricated in racial difference.[9] But recognizing this requires us to imagine forms of solidarity that do not reify empathy as a guiding principle. We should not have to understand others or hear their plights in terms that we can most easily absorb to be willing to fight the systems and structures and powers that bring them harm.

1   Teju Cole, "The White-Savior Industrial Complex," *The Atlantic*,
     March 21, 2012, https://www.theatlantic.com/international/
     archive/2012/03/the-white-savior-industrial-complex/254843/
     (accessed April 13, 2024).
2   Teju Cole (@tejucole), X, March 8, 2012, https://x.com/tejucole/
     status/1778095558608150529 (accessed April 10, 2024); https://x.
     com/tejucole/status/177810262223626241 (accessed April 10, 2024).
3   The description that follows draws upon my 2018 review of the
     installation of *Love Story* at Boston's Museum of Fine Arts, published
     in *4Columns*. See Aruna D'Souza, "Candice Breitz," *4Columns*,
     September 7, 2018, https://www.4columns.org/d-souza-aruna/
     candice-breitz (accessed April 13, 2024).
4   See Emily Watlington's review of *Love Story* in *The Brooklyn
     Rail*, November 7, 2018, https://brooklynrail.org/2018/07/artseen/
     CANDICE-BREITZLove-Story (accessed March 14, 2024).
5   "Global Trends Report," UNHCR (The UN Refugee Agency), June
     2023, https://www.unhcr.org/global-trends (accessed March 4, 2024).

6   "Print the Legend: Writing the Screenplay for Harriet," Focus
     Features, November 1, 2019, https://www.focusfeatures.com/
     article/interview_screenwriter_gregory-allen-howard (accessed
     April 13, 2024).

7   D'Souza, "Candice Breitz."

8   Josie Thaddeus-Johns, "Too Long, Didn't Read: Candice Breitz,"
     Elephant Magazine (Spring 2018).

9   I have explored the question of empathy's relation to race in other
     writings, including "'Open Casket' and the Question of Empathy,"
     Longreads, May 21, 2018, https://longreads.com/2018/05/21/
     open-casket-and-the-question-of-empathy/ (accessed April 10, 2024).
     Studies on racial bias when it comes to empathy are myriad—to
     the extent that it seems futile to cite just one. But one of the most
     striking is an investigation published in *Frontiers in Psychology*,
     which found that even when it came to the perception of other people's
     physical pain, racial bias plays a dismayingly significant role:
     "Empathy for pain is a source of deep emotional feelings and a strong
     trigger of pro-social behavior. ...[We] found that Caucasian observ-
     ers reacted to pain suffered by African people significantly less than
     to pain in Caucasian people." Matteo Forgiarini, Marcello Gallucci,
     and Angelo Maravita, "Racism and the Empathy for Pain on Our
     Skin," *Frontiers in Psychology* 2, no. 108 (May 23, 2011): 1, https://doi.
     org/10.3389/fpsyg.2011.00108.

III
Connecting through Opacity

The refusal of a politics that relies on empathy to build solidarity is, for people of the global majority especially, a matter of self-preservation. This is an argument that has been made, perhaps most generously and forcefully, by the Martinican poet and postcolonial theorist Édouard Glissant.

One of the key ideas in Glissant's *Poetics of Relation*, originally published in French in 1990, is that of the right to opacity.[1] The right to opacity stands in opposition to Western ontology's demand for transparency—a demand to know the other (whether an individual or a culture or, in fact, however otherness is being conceptualized in the moment). The West's need to know is never innocent curiosity, and rarely is it a simple desire for entanglement—it almost always takes place within a relationship of domination, and thus whatever knowledge results is essentially derived without real consent. Let's put this in tangible terms: one only has to think of how Europe's empire-building adventures were carried out not only with armies and navies but with cadres of recordkeepers, bureaucrats, artists, photographers, accountants, census takers, scientists, and botanists, all of whom were tasked with gathering information and categorizing both the resources and the people to whom they speciously laid claim. Glissant explains the Western imaginary as follows: "In order to understand and thus accept you, I have to measure your solidity with the ideal scale providing me with grounds to make comparisons and, perhaps, judgments. I have to reduce."[2]

When a postcolonial subject demands opacity, on the other hand, they are asserting the right to remain untranslatable into Western thought, the right to remain unrecorded by the colonizing institutions of the West, the right to remain irreducible to Western categorizations, and—most importantly for us—the right to remain unknown by the knowledge gatherers of the West. It is thus a fundamental prerequisite to equality and the ability to fully participate in the world. It is an idea that upends some of our most basic liberal notions of what it is to be in solidarity, as well—especially the idea of empathy, which is based on the seemingly benign notion of understanding. But "to understand" has a darker side, more apparent in French, where the word (*comprendre*) suggests something like "seizing" or "taking hold of." Empathy is not a necessary prerequisite for a common cause, Glissant insists: "To feel in solidarity with [the other] or to build with him or to like what he does, it is not necessary for me to grasp him. It is not necessary to try to become the other (to become other) nor to 'make' him in my image."[3]

In Manthia Diawara's 2010 film *Édouard Glissant: One World in Relation*, based on a series of interviews conducted with the writer while making a transatlantic voyage on the *Queen Mary II*, Glissant explains how this is possible—by talking about his relationship to broccoli:

> Everyone likes broccoli, but I hate it. But do I
> know why? Not at all. I accept my opacity on that
> level. Why wouldn't I accept it on other levels?
> Why wouldn't I accept the Other's opacity? Why
> must I absolutely understand the Other in order
> to live next to him and work with him? That's one
> of the laws of Relation. In Relation, elements don't
> blend just like that, don't lose themselves just
> like that. Each element can keep its—I won't just
> say its autonomy but also its essential quality.

But how might one move from acceptance to political solidarity while keeping everyone's right to opacity

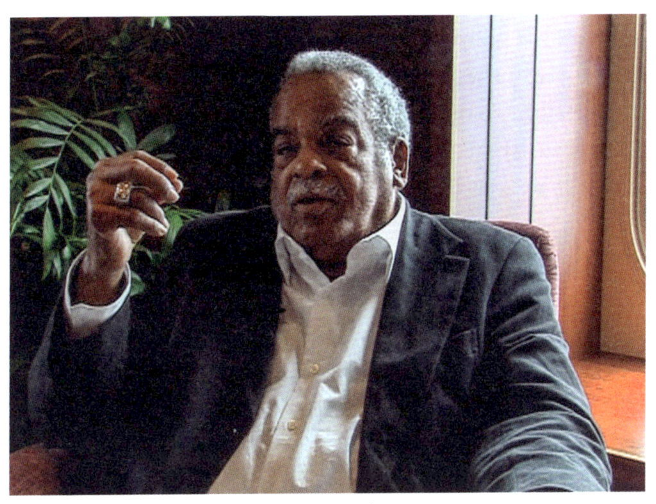

Édouard Glissant, in Manthia Diawara's *Édouard Glissant: one world in relation* (2010), video still

intact—while not demanding of the other that they justify or even explain themselves and their right to exist? Glissant tells a story that hints at what this form of encounter, which leaves the other's opacity intact, might look like. He describes being in Martinique and seeing a young man passing on the beach in front of his house. This young man, it was widely known, had withdrawn from the world of communication. Feeling that it isn't right to describe someone "so rigorously adrift," Glissant instead tries to show "the nature of his speechlessness":

I made an attempt to communicate with this absence. I respected his stubborn silence but (frustrated by my inability to make myself "understood" or accepted) wanted nonetheless to establish some system of relation with this walker that was not based on words. Since he went back and forth with the regularity of a metronome in front of the little garden between our house and the beach, one day I called him silently. I didn't exactly know what sign to make—it had to be something neither affected or condescending, but also not critical or distant. That time he didn't answer, but the second or third time around (since without being insistent I was insisting) he replied with a sign that was minute, at least to my eyes; for this gesture was perhaps the utmost he was capable of expressing: "I understand what you are attempting to undertake. You are trying to find out why I walk like this—not-here. I accept your trying. But look around and see if it's worth explaining. Are you, of yourself, worth my explaining this to you? So, let's leave it at that. We have gone as far as we can together." I was inordinately proud to have gotten this answer.[4]

How beautiful this is. I wonder what sort of solidarities and alliances we might form on the basis of such mutual respect, one in which we acknowledge our right not to translate ourselves into terms that another may understand. What are the tiny gestures, the boundaries, the mutual agreements to go only so far in our communication as to know communication has happened at all, that might make the possibility of moving toward a common cause possible? And, at the same time as respecting others' autonomy, how do we, people of the global majority, respect our own right to opacity? How do we act in political ways and form political alliances even as we refuse to participate in liberal culture's demands that we lay ourselves bare, justify our need for justice?

In 1995, I saw the Cuban-born artist Felix Gonzalez-Torres speak at the Institute of Fine Arts at New York University—my graduate school. He was brilliant despite the fact that his body was failing him (he would die

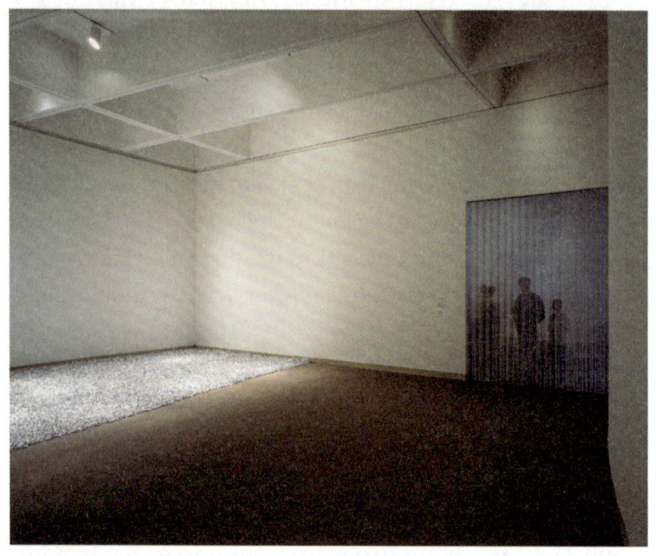

Installation view: *Felix Gonzalez-Torres: Traveling*, Hirshhorn Museum and Sculpture Garden, The Smithsonian Institution, Washington, DC, June 16–September 11, 1994

of AIDS only months later). He spoke of making work about queer love, queer bodies, and AIDS—in what was still the throes of the 1990s iteration of culture wars—and about his choice to speak, in some sense, in code, refusing to visualize identity but rather enacting a certain kind of relation within his work:

> When I had a show at the Hirshhorn, Senator [Ted] Stevens, who is one of the most homophobic anti-art senators, said he was going to come to the opening and I thought he's going to have a really hard time explaining to his constituency how pornographic and homoerotic two clocks side-by-side are. He came there looking for dicks and asses. There was nothing like that.[5]

No one, I think, can possibly look at Gonzalez-Torres's mirrors and clocks, at his slowly depleting candy spills, and not understand how completely these works are about his love for his partner, or about queer love more broadly, or about the grief and pain produced by the cultural and political homophobia that refused to treat the HIV/AIDS epidemic as a crisis because of a hatred for those whom the disease affected most. For the artist, though, there was a strategy in keeping his work ungraspable by or untranslatable into the vocabulary of hate wielded by right-wing culture warriors.[6] It allowed him the room to insist on being in the world, to not retreat into silence or disengagement, without being caught up in, or grasped by, a language he had never agreed to speak.

Working with similar themes, Stephanie Syjuco's 2019 video *Block Out the Sun* hinges on questions of the colonial subject's right to opacity. It is the result of the artist's research into the city archives of St. Louis, Missouri, which hosted the 1904 World's Fair. The exposition was mounted to celebrate two milestones: the centennial of the Louisiana Purchase, a watershed event in America's history as a settler-colonial nation, and the country's recent ascendancy (or perhaps devolution) into an imperial one. Only six years before, in 1898, after a series of military conflicts with Spain, the United States had signed the Treaty of Paris, which transferred a number of former Spanish colonies—including Puerto Rico, Cuba, Guam, and the Philippines—to its control. With these two acts—the violent seizure of land from Indigenous peoples in North America and another from people beyond its borders—a country borne out of resistance to British colonizers had become a colonizer in its own right.

One of the infamous features of the St. Louis fair was the Philippine Reservation, a forty-seven-acre "living exhibition" in which more than 1,000 Filipinos were forcibly removed from their homes half a continent away to

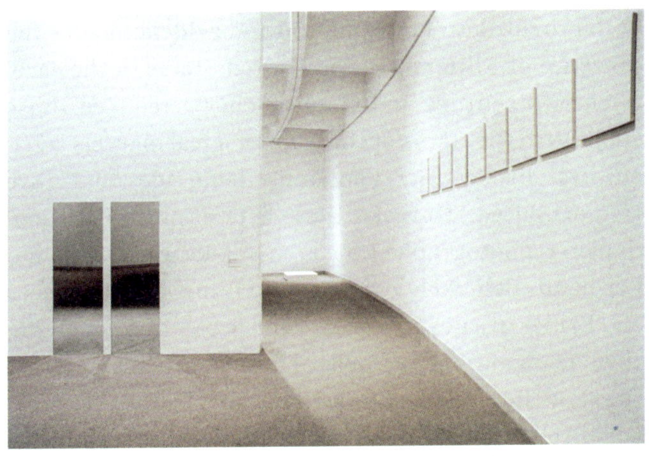

Installation view: *Felix Gonzalez-Torres: Traveling*, Hirshhorn Museum and Sculpture Garden, The Smithsonian Institution, Washington, DC, June 16–September 11, 1994

become a public display of American imperial power in Missouri. They were forced to construct their traditional village dwellings and live entirely in view of the fair's countless visitors. In sifting through the archives of this dubious project, Syjuco was confronted by images of the Philippine Reservation—photos taken by tourists, newspapers, fair organizers, and researchers—that both provided rare information and evidence about the presence of Filipinos in the United States in the early twentieth century and simultaneously reduced those subjects to the status of the technological marvels, agricultural displays, art, and amusement rides that were also exhibited. To resist these acts of objectification, Syjuco rephotographed the archival documents, laying her hands delicately over the unwilling subjects' faces and bodies in a gesture of care and protection, shielding them from our prying looks. The artist then assembled the shots into a five-minute video, in which still images advance with the sound of a shutter. With her protective gesture, Syjuco, who is Filipino American, offers the subjects of these photos a belated right to opacity that colonialism stripped away from them, and in doing so claims that opacity for their descendants, including those thrown into the diaspora in colonialism's wake.

I will offer one final example of the aesthetic and discursive possibilities of opacity. In the introduction to his book *Hungry Listening: Resonant Theory for Indigenous*

Sound Studies, Dylan Robinson, a xwélmexw (Stó:lō/ Skwah) artist, curator, and writer, tells the story of early encounters between Stó:lō people of the Pacific Northwest and white men who arrived in the late 1850s, during the gold rush.[7] The word used by the Stó:lō to describe these men was *xwelítem*, literally "starving person," referring to both the bodily state of deprivation in which they arrived and to their hunger for gold. By calling his book *Hungry Listening*, Robinson positions settler forms of listening, too, as a kind of voracious demand for transparency.

Among the topics Robinson treats are the ways in which museums, music venues, and academic study "make space" for Indigenous music and performance precisely by translating them into the terms of classical—European-derived—musical forms under the guise of multiculturalism or diversity, but in ways that are simply continuations of other forms of settler-colonialist extractivist logic. An instance of the latter may be, for example, museums that can only conceive of engaging with Native American art or performance by offering something that a larger, mostly white, audience can consume—rarely acknowledging the need for members of those communities to have space for discussing or transmitting ancestral, traditional, or in-group knowledge among themselves and providing museum resources accordingly.

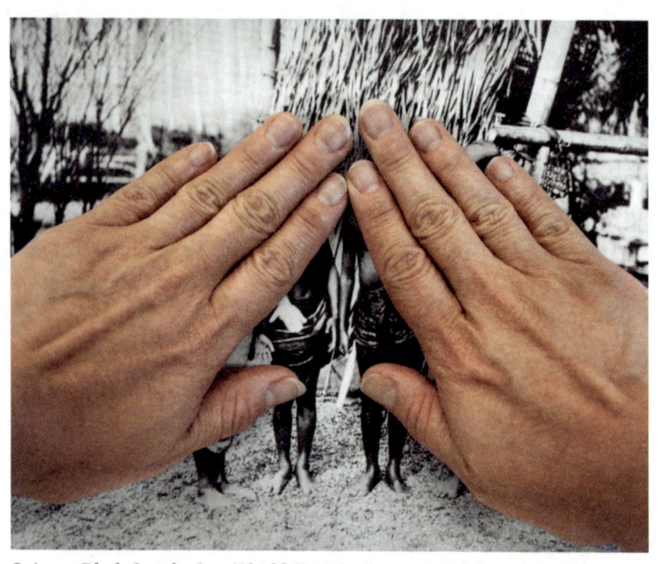

Syjuco, *Block Out the Sun (Shield)* (2019), photographic intervention

As part of the framing of his argument, and as a protective gesture toward his subject and parts of his audience, Robinson draws upon David Garneau's conceptualization of the "irreducible spaces of Aboriginality"—"gatherings, ceremony, Cree-only discussions, kitchen-table conversations, email exchanges, et cetera, in which Blackfootness, Métisness, and so on, are performed without settler attendance," not as "a show for others but a site where people simply are...without the sense that they are being witnessed by people who are not equal participants."[8] And so, a third of the way through the chapter, Robinson "affirms Indigenous sovereignty with the following injunction":

> If you are a non-Indigenous, settler, ally, or *xwelítem* reader, I ask that you stop reading by the end of this page. I hope that you will rejoin us for chapter one. ... The next section of the book, however, is written exclusively for Indigenous readers.[9]

The non-Indigenous reader has a choice, one that pushes back on our assumptions about the free flow of information, especially in our digital age: dive into those pages so as to understand the subject more completely or respect the call for sovereignty. I interviewed Robinson about the book when it was first launched, and he told me that a surprising number of people approached him to let him know that they appreciated the rhetorical gesture, but read the pages anyway, feeling it was only that—a rhetorical gesture. So deeply ingrained is the idea of the need for knowledge to be transparent that there was apparently no way of conceiving a situation in which it wouldn't be so.

To actually acknowledge the gambit as genuine and worthy of respect means, for many of us who read books like Robinson's to develop an understanding of cultures and communities with which we would like to ally ourselves and whose interests we would like to advance, letting go of our desire for transparency. It means, as Glissant imagines his beach walker to have communicated in that subtle, almost imperceptible gesture, that "[w]e have gone as far as we can together."[10] Such behavior does not prevent our treating those sovereign subjects with respect or fighting for justice on their behalf—but it does require us to cede our demands that they make themselves completely known to us in the process.

1   Édouard Glissant, *The Poetics of Relation*, trans. Betsy Wing (Ann Arbor: University of Michigan Press, 1997); see especially "For Opacity," 189–93.
2   Glissant, *The Poetics of Relation*, 190.
3   Glissant, *The Poetics of Relation*, 193.
4   Glissant, *The Poetics of Relation*, 122–23.
5   Gonzalez-Torres told this story many times; this quotation is taken from Theo Gordon, "Spit or Swallow? Orality in the Art of Felix Gonzalez-Torres," *Art History* 43, no. 4 (September 2020): 787.
6   The term "culture warrior" was claimed as a descriptor by right-wing participants in the culture wars in the last decade of the twentieth century, enough so that the Fox News commentator Bill O'Reilly used the term as the title of a 2006 book that outlined what he saw as his righteous fight against the "secular-progressive" agenda.
7   Dylan Robinson, *Hungry Listening: Resonant Theory for Indigenous Sound Studies* (Minneapolis: University of Minnesota Press, 2020).
8   Quoted in Robinson, *Hungry Listening*, 24.
9   Robinson, *Hungry Listening*, 25.
10 Glissant, *The Poetics of Relation*, 123.

IV
Leaving Difference Intact

Though the term "intersectional feminism" has existed since 1989, when legal scholar Kimberlé Crenshaw coined the phrase, it has been over the past decade that the idea has been held up as a new basis on which to conceive of possible political alliances.[1] It allows for a truly feminist politics that might address interests and demands beyond those of white, bourgeois, cis women: not just abortion access, but a mother's right to raise her children without the state taking them away; not just equal pay for equal work, but a living wage; not just access to birth control, but access to hormone therapy for trans people; not just the ability to free oneself from domestic drudgery, but affordable, nondiscriminatory housing; not just the opportunity to break the corporate glass ceiling, but the need to dismantle capitalism; not just the rejection of patriarchy, but the rejection of racism and imperialism, which are both its motor and its consequence.

However, only since the election of Donald Trump in 2016—who received 53 percent of white women's votes—have mainstream feminists in the United States, mainly white, largely middle-class, and often aligned with the Democratic Party, become acutely aware of the need to form solidarities across ever-deepening chasms of race, class, and other markers of unequal treatment. The scramble to "become intersectional" has played out in public over the last decade, as these feminist groups have tried to reimagine themselves in more inclusive ways. (One might recall, for example, the initial fumbles around the Women's March on Washington, DC, on January 21, 2017, when, after an outcry, a number of women of color activists were added to the organizational team.[2])

The problem with this mindset of opening mainstream feminism to intersectional concerns, of course, is that it is conceived as an act of generosity—a making-welcome of difference, a function of empathy and goodwill—in which the center makes room for those at the margins. It is a "big tent" approach, which dreams of consensus, common purpose, and indivisibility. But intersectionality as a political strategy isn't an act of generosity, a product of empathy, or an understanding across the expanses of difference—it is a survival strategy, a necessary response to a political and social landscape in which acts of resistance are too easily co-opted, rendered powerless, made illegal, marketed to death, or otherwise subverted. It approaches feminism as a matter of coalition building and collaboration across difference and thereby leaves difference intact, abandoning the hope for a unified voice because it sees the many, sometimes conflicting and contradictory, positions as the most effective way to undermine the maddening single-mindedness of white supremacist, capitalist patriarchy. It is rooted, most crucially, in an explosion of the center, of rendering untenable the notion of margins.

An exhibition at A.I.R. Gallery in New York in 1980, *Dialectics of Isolation: An Exhibition of Third World Women Artists of the United States*, curated by Ana Mendieta, Kazuko Miyamoto, and Zarina Hashmi, gives us another view into the kind of imperfect, shifting solidarities for which I have been advocating in these pages.[3] The exhibition was an oppositional gesture. It grew out of a contemporary and widespread critique of A.I.R. Gallery, the eponymous journal published by the feminist Heresies Collective, and other women-centered cultural organizations whose programming and activism largely reflected the concerns of their mostly white, middle-class membership, to the chagrin of many women of color in the art world. But *Dialectics of Isolation* was not predicated on the idea of inclusion—that is, its goal seems not to have been to merely make space for artists of color in a hitherto white space, though it certainly achieved that. Rather, it was a much more radical idea: the productive value of difference, the power of speaking from a position of isolation. "As non-white women our struggles are two-fold," Mendieta wrote in the introduction to the catalogue. "This exhibition points not necessarily to the injustice or incapacity of a society that has not been willing to include us, but more towards a personal will to continue being 'other.'"[4]

The challenge Mendieta and her cocurators posed to their peers at A.I.R. and other feminist art spaces in New York was contained in the title of the show, referring as it did to the idea of "Third World women." The use of the term "Third World" to denote United States–based women of color emerged over the course of the 1970s; it drew upon a Cold War term that referred to mostly developing nations in the Global South that resisted alignment with the global superpowers of the NATO alliance (the First World) and the Communist Bloc (the Second World). The embrace of the idea of a Third World feminism came as Black, Chicanx, Indigenous, and other feminists of color in the United States recognized the importance of seeing their own liberation as part of larger, global processes of decolonization and linked to anti-imperialist struggles such as the South African Anti-Apartheid Movement, independence movements in former colonies, and

Ana Mendieta, "Introduction," in *Dialectics of Isolation: An Exhibition of Third World Women Artists of the United States* (1980), catalog page antipoverty activism. By theorizing the existence of the Third World within the First, they were able to critique the class and race privilege of Western feminism and see their own oppression as a continued legacy of colonialism and its multiple forms of violence. It was predicated not on a univocal, big-tent notion of feminism but on strategic coalition building through shared interests.

For those who took on the mantle of Third World feminism, an anti-racist feminism was not just one flavor among many to choose from in the fight against patriarchy; it was, on the contrary, a fundamental and necessary starting point. As Barbara Smith, one of the founding members of the Combahee River Collective, a Black feminist group that became widely influential in art world conversations thanks to their challenge to the journal *Heresies* for not including a single Black person in their 1977 issue on lesbian art and artists, wrote:

> The reason racism is a feminist issue is easily
> explained by the inherent definition of feminism.
> Feminism is the political theory and practice
> to free all women: women of color, working class
> women, poor women, physically challenged
> women, lesbians, old women, as well as white
> economically privileged heterosexual women.
> Anything less than this is not feminism but
> merely female self-aggrandizement.[5]

In their famous 1977 statement, one that is largely credited as the origins of a rigorous, class-conscious, intersectional form of identity politics, the Combahee River Collective outlined the expansiveness of their notion of feminism:

> The inclusiveness of our politics makes us concerned with any situation that impinges upon the lives of women, Third World and working people.... We might, for example, become involved in workplace organizing at a factory that employs Third World Women or picket a hospital that is cutting back on already inadequate health care to a Third World community, or set up a rape crisis center in a Black neighborhood. Organizing around welfare and daycare concerns might also be a focus. The work to be done and the countless issues that this work represents merely reflect the pervasiveness of our oppression.[6]

The multiplicity embodied in Third World feminism—not simply the various identities, races, ethnicities, and colonial conditions of its adherents, but also the issues it understood to be central to its struggle—is reflected, perhaps, in the unusually emphatic heterogeneity of *Dialectics of Isolation*. The critic Carrie Rickey, in her review of the show in the *Village Voice*, saw this heterogeneity as a sort of incoherence, in which works she deemed to be "phenomenological" and "lyrical" stood in jarring contrast to the "ideological" art on view. Rickey attributed this disjuncture to what she saw as an emerging genre of exhibitions—the "affinity show"—that substituted an emphasis on "political and social considerations" for aesthetic ones.[7] She mapped out the exhibition's two poles (phenomenological-lyrical versus ideological) in surprisingly formal terms, however: abstraction versus representation, roughly speaking. As such, Rickey imposed an opposition on the works on view. On one side were Beverly Buchanan's grouping of cement blocks; Zarina's delicate, geometric, cast-paper reliefs; Lydia Okamura's site-specific installation, which involved painting the wall and floor of the gallery space to render the difference between horizontal and vertical planes moot; Senga Nengudi's weighted pantyhose sculptures with their uncanny corporeality; and Selena W. Persico's conceptual rendering of the landscape as a site of decay and degeneration. On the other side, we had Howardena Pindell's iconic video *Free, White, and 21* (1980), in which she dons white drag to recount shocking, real-life encounters with liberal white feminists; Janet Olivia Henry's playful, hilarious, and devastating *Ju Ju Bag* (1979–80), which contains the necessary, if miniaturized, accoutrements of the WPM (white Protestant male); and work by the Los Angeles–based Chicana muralist Judith Baca.

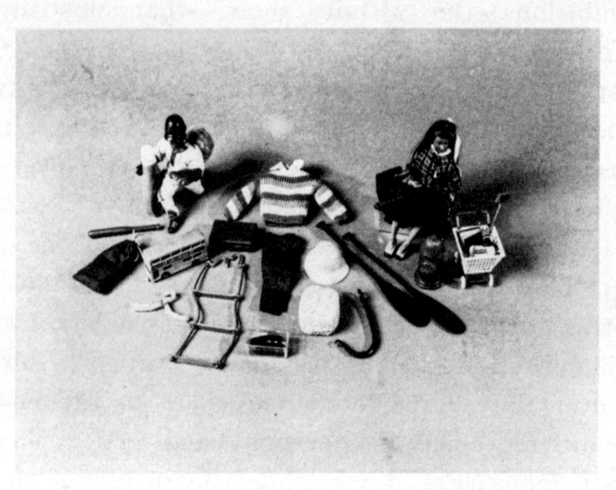

Janet Olivia Henry, *Juju Box for a White Protestant Male* (1979–1980), catalog page

In her search for cohesion, Rickey's otherwise entirely sympathetic and sensitive review missed the point of how affinity might operate in curatorial terms: as a cognate, we might say, for the tactical idea of coalitions that Third World feminism sought—as a matter of shared concerns across formal and conceptual divides, in ways that keep such divides intact but see their dialectical and productive potential. Buchanan's cast-concrete blocks were as site-specific as, for example, both Okamura's installation and Baca's *Great Wall of Los Angeles* (1978). Buchanan made her concrete admixture out of local materials and often placed her blocks outdoors to mark sites or events significant in the Black American experience.[8] Buchanan's and Zarina's reimagining of Minimalism's formal language was as much an upending of white masculinity, it seems to me, as Henry's parodic lexicon—both minimalism and preppy fashion being largely the purview of white Protestant males. Nengudi's use of pantyhose, weighted, bulging, and stretched, to refer to the ways colored bodies are stressed and pulled apart in a racist world is echoed in Pindell's video, in which, in addition to appearing in whiteface to act out the words of various "allies" she has encountered in her life, she pulls a stocking over her head, disfiguring her face in an attempt to mask her Blackness. Baca's and Okamura's interventions both turn to architectural space in order to introduce otherness, to make present bodies that have been absented from the public representation of community—Okamura's in terms of pure (skin) color, Baca's in terms of narrative representation of missing histories. There are more connections to be teased out, to be sure. In short: *Dialectics of Isolation* can be understood as an incohesive show only if one fails to look for the more subtle, glancing ways in which these artists' works share conceptual and political terrain.

Dialectics of Isolation offers a set of timely reminders for our politically volatile moment, a moment in which we are struggling to find effective models of organizing and protest to counter increasingly bald expressions of racism and misogyny in our social and political worlds, and in which art institutions (from small independent spaces to large museums) are being challenged to make clear their own complicity and investments in structural racism, sexism, colonialism, and capitalism. First, the exhibition is a reminder to mainstream feminist organizers that models for intersectional feminism have long existed within the spheres of Black and woman-of-color feminisms, most pertinently as Third World feminism. In other words, a truly intersectional feminism is not an expansion of liberal white feminism but a decentering of it. Second, it offers a historical model for the idea of decolonization—a concept that has gained currency in the art world in recent years, driving many provocations for institutions to reimagine themselves in relation to everything from Indigenous land claims, to repatriation of stolen objects in museum collections, to gentrification. And third—and perhaps most importantly—*Dialectics of Isolation* offers a model for how such political imperatives can be translated into curatorial form, through an exhibition that privileges difference and highlights the less obvious correspondences of works that share a broadly sympathetic terrain and come together to speak in unexpected, mutually reinforcing ways. The open-endedness of Mendieta, Kazuko, and Zarina's show conjured a space of multiplicity, one that transformed A.I.R. Gallery and, by eschewing curatorial models of "coherence," forced us to see affinity in surprising and politically efficacious ways.

1   The concept, however, originates even further back, since Black feminists and other feminists of color began calling for an expansion of white feminism's relatively narrow focus. Kimberlé Crenshaw, "Demarginalizing the Intersection of Race and Sex: A Black Feminist Critique of Antidiscrimination Doctrine, Feminist Theory, and Antiracist Politics," *University of Chicago Legal Forum* 140, no. 1 (1989): 139–67; Crenshaw, "Mapping the Margins: Intersectionality, Identity Politics, and Violence against Women of Color," *Stanford Law Review* 43, no. 6 (July 1991): 1241–99.

2   On the question of intersectionality and the Women's March, see, for example, Farah Stockman, "Women's March on Washington Opens Contentious Dialogues about Race," *The New York Times*, January 9, 2017, https://www.nytimes.com/2017/01/09/us/womens-march-on-washington-opens-contentious-dialogues-about-race.html (accessed April 13, 2024).

3   I have benefited from the work of Anastasia Tuazon, and I thank
     her for sharing it with me. See Anastasia Tuazon, "The Dialectics of
     Isolation: Third World Women Artists Form a Coalition through
     Difference" (master's thesis, Stony Brook University, 2018).
4   "Introduction," in *Dialectics of Isolation: An Exhibition of Third World
     Women Artists in the United States*, exh. cat. A.I.R. Gallery (New York,
     1980), n.p.
5   From a talk Barbara Smith gave at the closing session at the National
     Women's Studies Association Conference, May 1979; published as
     Barbara Smith, "Racism and Women's Studies," *Frontiers: A Journal
     of Women's Studies* 5, no. 1 (1980): 48–49, and reprinted in *All the
     Women Are White, All the Blacks Are Men, But Some of Us Are Brave:
     Black Women's Studies*, ed. Gloria T. Hull et al. (New York: Feminist
     Press at CUNY, 1982), 49.
6   The Combahee River Collective, "A Black Feminist Statement,"
     in *We Wanted a Revolution*, 176 and 182. First published in Zillah
     R. Eisenstein, ed., *Capitalist Patriarchy and the Case for Socialist
     Feminism* (New York: Monthly Review Press, 1979).
7   Carrie Rickey, "The Passion of Ana," *Village Voice*, September 10–16,
     1980, 75.
8   See my review of the exhibition *Beverly Buchanan – Ruins and Rituals*,
     Brooklyn Museum, October 21, 2016 – March 5, 2017: Aruna
     D'Souza, "Beverly Buchanan," *4Columns*, November 4, 2016, http://
     www.4columns.org/d-souza-aruna/beverly-buchanan (accessed
     April 14, 2024).

Coda
Care before Love

What if we imagined a form of political solidarity that was not based on empathy but on its opposite—on imperfect solidarity; a solidarity defined by its respect for opacity? Are there ways to sit with the unknowability of the other and still care for and with them, without translating ourselves into their terms? Are there ways to understand the world outside of the binaries of self and other, instead embracing the fundamental interconnectedness of human (and, in this time of environmental collapse, nonhuman) life? What would it mean if our politics were based not on our ability to empathize with people whose experiences are distant from our own, but on our willingness to care for others just by virtue of their being *beings*?

A decade ago, desperate for a pet, my child convinced me to get them a chameleon. Now, chameleons are the most impossible creatures to anthropomorphize—which is to say they are hard to imagine in human terms. They're like little dinosaurs, their only "emotions" are fear and not fear, they don't recognize you or acknowledge you or perceive you as anything but a predator who occasionally provides them with food. After a few weeks of acquiring this chameleon, feeding him disgusting live crickets every day, having him hiss and snap at them anytime they got near him, not even being able to watch him because he was always hiding in the foliage, my kid came down from their room. "I love Beppe"—that was the chameleon's name, Cesare Beppe The Rock Johnson the Third Sedita, in fact—"I love him so much!" "Love him?" I asked. "How can you love him? He doesn't seem to be very loveable." "But Mom," they said to me, in all their twelve-year-old wisdom. "I've been keeping him alive for all this time. I've been taking care of him. How can you not end up loving something that you have to take care of?"

And then there's another story, about my mother, an anesthesiologist born and raised in India, who was bitten by a dog as a child and grew up with a healthy disdain for the beasts. She gave in to the relentless entreaties of her husband and two children over the years—we adopted a series of dogs, farm dogs, all problematic in certain ways because of their treatment early in life. As is often the case, despite her kids' promises to be the ones seeing to the dogs' basic needs and love them with all our hearts, we failed at the first pledge, succeeding only at the second. It was left to my dog-averse, extremely put-upon mom to take up the slack. She fed them, took care of their medical needs (including, for one, repeatedly anesthetizing him so she could remove the porcupine quills from his face, the result of an ongoing grudge that eventually killed him). Every once in a while, I would see her sitting on the porch, giving one of the dogs a pat and feeding him a little bit of whatever she was snacking on, but I instinctively knew it didn't come out of love or anything like empathy. It came, quite straightforwardly, out of an obligation to care. And that care was, in fact, more significant than all the love my sister, father, and I ever showed those dogs.

Care before love—or care before empathy: this is the politics I aspire to. A solidarity that comes very directly from a commitment to care *because that is the most basic obligation we have toward each other*. If empathy or love develop along the way, that is a gift, but not a requirement. Care is an outward-directed action; love and empathy are too caught up in the ego to be given freely. (There is no such thing as unconditional love, I firmly believe.) The obligation to care is what I saw my parents act upon in relation to every patient they treated—Mom was an anesthesiologist, as I mentioned, and Dad was a surgeon—even the ones in our redneck town in rural Alberta who hurled racial slurs at them; my dad garnered unwanted fame in our province for reattaching a man's severed arm, but we were the only ones who knew he did it despite being called the worst possible racial epithet by this man.

Care is infinitely harder than love, because it often requires us to act in spite of our empathy, rather than because of it—it requires us to place the cause of justice ahead of our own feelings. But the solidarities it creates, even the precarious ones, even those that arise only momentarily before other, shifting alliances unfold, are the solidarities that focus on what needs to be done collectively. Modeling this—not only in our political praxis, but in our writing, our art making, our curating—allows us to reimagine the terms of how and why we come together, clearing a space for real transformation.

Acknowledgments

Even a short book like this, which has developed over time and in overlapping ways, can be understood as a kind of map of relationships and encounters, of moments of epiphany with friends and colleagues, and of hard work with editors and publishers. I'd like to thank Aaron Bogart for inviting me to write it, and for giving me a prompt to start. In addition to these, the following people and organizations have supported my work and inspired my musings: Dushko Petrovitch; Jill Casid; Lorelei Stewart, Karen Greenwalt, and Katja Rivera; Steven Nelson and the Center for Advanced Studies in the Visual Arts, where I was in residence as the Edmond J. Safra Visiting Professor in 2022; the participants in 2022's Safra Colloquium, including Anthony Elms, Raven Chacon, Candice Hopkins, Kandis Williams, and Stephanie Syjuco; the members of South Asian Feminist Futures; Carin Kuoni, Laura Raicovich, Amar Kanwar, Natalie Diaz, Kameelah Jahan Rasheed, and Chlöe Bass, key interlocutors in the Vera List Center's project "Studies into Darkness" in 2020; the institutions who invited me to talk through many of the ideas in this book; Candice Breitz; Anthony Aziz and Sammy Cucher; Judith Rodenbeck; Nizan Shaked; Emily Jacir; Siddhartha Mitter; and the thinkers and commentators on social media whose posts about what's happening in the world have made me think harder and deeper, for better and worse, about how to act in relation to others. And most of all, to Priya D'Souza McDonough, my fierce warrior of a child, who teaches me every day how a new generation is aspiring to change the world.

Biography

Aruna D'Souza is a writer and critic based in New York. She is a regular contributor to the *New York Times* and *4Columns*, where she is a member of the editorial advisory board. Her writing has also appeared in the *Wall Street Journal*, CNN.com, *Bookforum*, *Frieze*, *Momus*, and *Art in America*, among others. Her book, *Whitewalling: Art, Race, and Protest in 3 Acts* (Badlands Unlimited), was named one of the best art books of 2018 by the *New York Times*. She is the recipient of the 2021 Rabkin Prize for art journalism and a 2019 Andy Warhol Foundation Art Writers Grant.

Credits

"Empathy and Translation" was first printed, in modified form, in *Studies into Darkness: The Perils and Promise of Freedom of Speech*, ed. Carin Kuoni and Laura Raicovich (Amherst, MA: Amherst College Press, 2022). The essay traces its origins to my introduction for the volume *Art History in the Wake of the Global Turn*, ed. Jill Casid and Aruna D'Souza (New Haven, CT: Yale University Press, 2014); "*Sea of Poppies* and the Possibilities of Mistranslation," in *Traduttore, Traditore*, ed. Karen Greenwalt and Katja Rivera, exh. cat. Gallery 400 (Chicago: University of Illinois at Chicago, 2017); and a lecture, "Empathy Will Not Save Us," at the Creative Time Summit X in New York on January 31, 2020.

"Empathy and Whiteness" draws from "The Problem of Whiteness," in *Candice Breitz: Labor: Catalogue Raisonné* (Bonn: Kunstmuseum Bonn and Snoeck, 2020).

Sections of "Opacity" were first delivered as a lecture at the Center for Advanced Studies in the Visual Arts at the National Gallery in Washington, DC, where I was in residence as the Edmond J. Safra Visiting Professor in 2022. It also draws briefly upon "Escaping the Archive's Gaze," in *Stephanie Syjuco: After/Images*, exh. cat. Frye Art Museum (Seattle, 2024).

"Leaving Difference Intact" was first published as "Curating Difference," in *Dialectics of Entanglement: Do We Exist Together?*, exh. cat. A.I.R. Gallery (New York, 2018). It draws upon my essay "Early Intersections: The Work of Third World Feminism," which appeared in *We Wanted a Revolution: Black Radical Women, 1965–85: New Perspectives*, ed. Catherine Morris and Rujeko Hockley (New York: Brooklyn Museum, 2018).

Image Credits

P. 11
Screenshot of Instagram story by Kameelah Jahan Rasheed, February 2024, taken by the author

P. 18
Participants in a blockade by the Extinction Rebellion climate movement at the start of the Block Berlin action week lie on the ground in sleeping bags at the Großer Stern, with "Make empathy great again" written on the ground. October 7, 2019 © picture alliance/dpa; Photo: Christoph Soeder

P. 32
Three lascars on the P&O liner RMS *Viceroy of India*, 1930–1939, cellulose acetate negative; Marine Photo Service, image via National Maritime Museum from Greenwich, United Kingdom, Wikimedia Commons, no known copyright restrictions

P. 43
Candice Breitz, *Love Story* (2016), featuring Julianne Moore and Alec Baldwin. Interviewee: Mamy Maloba Langa, 7-channel installation; Commissioned by the National Gallery of Victoria (Melbourne), Outset Germany (Berlin), and the Medienboard Berlin-Brandenburg

P. 44
Candice Breitz, *Love Story* (2016), featuring Julianne Moore and Alec Baldwin. Interviewee: José Maria João, 7-channel installation; Commissioned by the National Gallery of Victoria (Melbourne), Outset Germany (Berlin), and the Medienboard Berlin-Brandenburg

P. 55
Manthia Diawara, *Édouard Glissant: one world in relation* (2010), video still; Courtesy of the artist and Maumaus/Lumiar Cité

P. 58
Installation view: *Felix Gonzalez-Torres: Traveling*, Hirshhorn Museum and Sculpture Garden, The Smithsonian Institution, Washington, DC, June 16–September 11, 1994. Co-organized by Amada Cruz, Ann Goldstein, and Susanne Ghez. (Second venue of *Felix Gonzalez-Torres: Traveling*. Museum of Contemporary Art [MOCA], Los Angeles, CA. 24 Apr.–19 Jun. 1994.) From left: *"Untitled" (Placebo)*, 1991; *"Untitled" (Chemo)*, 1991. © Estate Felix Gonzalez-Torres, courtesy Felix Gonzalez-Torres Foundation

P. 61
Installation view: *Felix Gonzalez-Torres: Traveling*, Hirshhorn Museum and Sculpture Garden, The Smithsonian Institution, Washington, DC, June 16–September 11, 1994. Co-organized by Amada Cruz, Ann Goldstein and Susanne Ghez. (Second venue of *Felix Gonzalez-Torres: Traveling*. Museum of Contemporary Art [MOCA], Los Angeles, CA. 24 Apr.–19 Jun. 1994.) From left: *"Untitled" (Orpheus, Twice)*, 1991; *"Untitled" (Double Portrait)*, 1991; *"Untitled" (31 Days of Bloodworks)*, 1991. © Estate Felix Gonzalez-Torres, courtesy Felix Gonzalez-Torres Foundation

P. 64
Stephanie Syjuco, *Block Out the Sun (Shield)* (2019), photographic intervention in the archives of the Missouri Historical Society, archival pigment print mounted on aluminum, 15 × 20 in.; Courtesy of the artist, Catharine Clark Gallery, RYAN LEE Gallery, and Silverlens Gallery

P. 72
Ana Mendieta, "Introduction," *Dialectics of Isolation: An Exhibition of Third World Women Artists of the United States* (1980), catalog; Courtesy of A.I.R. Gallery and Fales Library and Special Collections, New York University

P. 76
Janet Olivia Henry, *Juju Box for a White Protestant Male* (1979–1980), mixed media; Courtesy of A.I.R. Gallery and Fales Library and Special Collections, New York University; Photo: Larry Brown

Colophon

Series editor:
Aaron Bogart

Copyediting:
Louisa Elderton

Editorial assistance:
Jude Macannuco

Proofreading:
Nadia Egan

Graphic design:
Daniela Burger

Typesetting:
Vreni Knödler

Typeface:
Kelvin Avec Clair

Printing:
druckhaus köthen

Paper:
F-color Karton Feinkorn,
Munken Print White

Published by
Floating Opera Press
Hasenheide 9
10967 Berlin
www.floatingoperapress.com

ISBN 978-3-9823894-8-6

Printed in Germany